Spring in the Ruined City

DU FU

Spring in the Ruined City
Selected Poems

Translated by Jonathan Waley

Calligraphy by Kaili Fu

Shearsman Books
Exeter

Published in the United Kingdom in 2008 by
Shearsman Books Ltd
58 Velwell Road
Exeter EX4 4LD

www.shearsman.com

ISBN 978-1-84861-000-2

Cover: *Mid-Autumn Festival* by Liu Guosong (born 1932). China,
1969. Hanging scroll, ink and colors on paper. The Avery Brundage
Collection, 2003.22. © Asian Art Museum of San Francisco. Used
by permission of the artist and of the Asian Art Museum of San
Francisco.

Acknowledgements
Some of these poems originally appeared in *Agenda* and *South-West
Arts*. My thanks to the editors.

I am grateful to my editor, Tony Frazer, for advice and comments.
I am also grateful to Nathalie Young and Jerome Betts for their
helpful comments. And I owe an enormous debt to Diana Gittins,
for her caring and constant encouragement and support, and her
deeply helpful comments.

Errata
On page 37, 6th (upper) column: for 遇 read 偶

On page 57, 2nd (upper) column: for 壯 read 牀

Contents

INTRODUCTION

This selection of Du Fu's poems concentrates on the ten years of his life[1] during which the Tang dynasty (618–907 AD) was very nearly overturned by rebellion, and Du Fu himself experienced great physical and emotional hardship. It is also the period when he began to write his greatest poems, and the range given here aims to demonstrate at least some of the qualities for which he is so famous.

The poems (and the notes on them in the Appendix) chronicle a definite movement from the bleak depression in the earlier verses, written in northern China during the near-fatal rebellion mentioned above, to a more hopeful note as the military tide turned[2], to a whole variety of moods, inspired by such stimuli as the lush landscapes of southern China[3] or his increasing despair that yet more disturbances (in effect, local rebellions) had broken out.

Du Fu put a great deal of his life and times into his poetry—indeed, much of the information we have about him is derived from his own writings. His response to such extreme times was itself extreme, not only in terms of emotion expressed, but also in terms of artistic achievement. In other words, this emergency (of the Tang dynasty) drove him to express himself with yet more urgency and innovatory daring. This is to be seen in particular in his handling of the eight-line verse form[4]. Bearing in mind, then, the historical context, much of what Du Fu says, and why he says it, should be fairly obvious—he gives his opinions freely, after all. The reader who would like more detail (perhaps more

---

[1] 755 to a little after 763 AD; the date of some of these last poems is not precisely certain. For more details on dates and background, see Contextual Background and Appendix, pp 96-100.

[2] See 'The Great Trek North', p38.

[3] where he moved after 759. There is more on this in the Contextual Background on pages 96-97.

[4] (technically known as lü-shi, ie regulated verse). This is discussed in more detail on the next page.

certainty) is advised to turn to pages 96–100, where there is an overview of events, which is followed by notes on individual poems.

Without doubt, he was a great risk-taker, in his life[5] as well as in his art. And there is a very real sense in which both the long poems given here—'Five Hundred Words' and 'The Great Trek North'[6]—which are considered among his greatest, bring out these qualities very clearly. In them Du Fu explores as fully as he can the potentialities of travelling, so that the journeying is metaphorical as well as literal; he also explores and celebrates his different moods, which ranged from near despair to near triumph. And with all this he combines vehement protest on social issues. It is hardly surprising that Du Fu's career as an official was extremely modest, and that he later (again, during the time-frame of these poems) abandoned such aspirations altogether. He was almost certainly too outspoken, and too original, to be awarded real power. Indeed, at one point during this period his outspokenness so angered the emperor that friends had to plead for his forgiveness.

The translations given here aim to re-create the huge variety, vigour, and passion of his work. Any translator also has to confront the more daring, innovatory tendencies evident in some of his four- and eight-line poems[7]. These poems are well known for the extent to which the images in them combine and contrast to make most of the meaning of the poem. To put it rather simply, in a poetic tradition where concrete images abound, the images in these poems almost work overtime, with the result that they begin to appear more important than the statements which would normally bind them together. An example of this is to be found in 'Spring View' (p32), where the first two lines run, literally

---

[5] This is probably less true of the earlier part of his life, when he cultivated various important people in the hope that this would encourage official advancement.

[6] Pages 14 and 38 respectively.

[7] That is, those on pages 32, 68, 70, 84, 86, 88.

GUO	PO	SHAN	HE	ZAI
state	shattered	mountains	rivers	remain

CHENG	CHUN	CAO	MU	SHEN
city	spring	grasses	trees	deep.

This careful vertical balancing (state/city// shattered/spring etc) is obviously part of the whole unit of sense, which works vertically as well as horizontally, and is (usually) in Chinese poetry not one line, but the couplet. And whilst this had usually been limited to the middle couplets of such eight-line, 'regulated verse' forms, Du Fu goes further, in the way he uses them in the first couplet (as here) or the last couplets as well. Often he implies much more through juxtaposed images than he actually states[8]. This is seen in lines 5 and 6 of the poem quoted (see p33), where

Look-out beacons   flash fire for months
Letter from home   would be gold

obviously contrast carefully. One might say that Du Fu pinpoints his emotional position with a kind of geographical accuracy.

When translating these poems, I felt the very strong images pulling apart within the line, which is why in my translation I broke up the lines in these poems. There is always a small tendency in this direction anyway, as much Chinese poetry up to this time has a caesura after the second or fourth syllable in five- and seven-syllable lines, respectively. This creates a mini-break in the meaning (and also, often, in the grammar). True, there are eight-liners (and four-liners too) where I have not separated the lines in this way. My reason for this is that a poem such as 'Spring Night in the Imperial Palace', or 'Two Verses Written by the Serpentine' (pages 58 and 59) contain more statement,

---

[8] In fact, this is common in much Chinese poetry. Du Fu, though, carried this further than his predecessors.

and are less imagistically 'strong', than 'Spring View' (already discussed) or 'This Wearisome Night' (p86), and this is equally true of the two series of quatrains on spring: those on p72–77 are clearly far more discursive and less tight than those on p84.

Readers may have encountered other leading poets of the Tang dynasty (618–907 AD), such as Li Po, Po Chu-yi and Li Shang-yin, to name just a few. It would be tedious (indeed, pointless) to enumerate the virtues of these poets without detailed examples of their work. However, this was indeed a period of great self-assurance, innovation and achievement by many gifted poets, and poetry was celebrated as an art-form, by its audiences as much as its practitioners, as never before. More prosaically, the relative stability of this dynasty—the country was united under one ruler for the first time in roughly four hundred years—enabled many poets to practise and refine their craft, building (in some respects) on the achievements of their predecessors.

What is extraordinary about Du Fu, though, is his ability to take us through the whole range of human emotions[9], from the peaks of excitement or joy to the depths of despair, from the deeply earnest to a light-heartedness which flirts with frivolity; and to do this whilst simultaneously reacting to his own position as someone living through his eventful times. It is no exaggeration to say that he lived his times through his poetry, with an intensity and an artistry which other Tang poets rarely achieved. These qualities, combined with the ability to handle, and greatly enhance, all the forms of verse then current, are the qualities which Chinese readers most admire in him—and have admired for the last 1,200 years.

It is the aim of these translations to convey at least something of the subtlety, vigour and versatility of Du Fu's poetry.

---

[9] Sometimes within a single poem, as in 'Five Hundred Words' (14) and 'The Great Trek North' (38)

NOTE ON TRANSLITERATION

Chinese names have mostly been represented in English by the Pinyin system. This is the official system used by the Chinese government, and has the obvious advantage of being accessible via any material on the Chinese language (Mandarin) or modern books on China itself. I have, however, followed the practice of Western authors in falling back on familiar spellings already well established in English: so the great river of southern China is (still) the Yangtze, (rather than the Yangzi, as in pinyin), and the other famous Tang poets mentioned on the facing page have enjoyed similar treatment. I have extended this licence to "Chiang", as in ('Three Poems written at Chiang Village', page 54), as the proper pinyin letter here is a Q (see below). I have found from my own practice, and through reading the translations of others, that odd-looking names, especially those which do not lend themselves to an immediate pronunciation in today's English, are just about the surest way to dam the flow of almost any line of verse[10].

Having said all of the above, the three letters used in pinyin which are most obviously different from what an English reader might expect are:

c: using pinyin, the musician Fats Waller would have spelt his name Fac Waller. So a word like 'cao', meaning grasses, starts with an aspirated 'ts' sound.

x: a 'sh' sound but with the tongue far lower in the mouth than in English. To approximate this, say 'see', then lower tongue/bring it forward until you get a 'sh' sound.

q: used to make a 'ch' sound in exactly the same position as the x-sound above.

---

[10] This is why, in some instances, I have paraphrased where (for instance) Du Fu's original text used a Chinese name for symbolic purposes. In line 4 of the first poem, on p14, for instance, the original text names two 'sage rulers'; Du's point, however, that in this (fantasy) role he is a most definitely a flop, is unaltered.

Du Fu

Selected Poems

杜
甫
詩
選

FIVE HUNDRED WORDS:
My Feelings on my Journey from the Capital to Fengxian.

Introduction

An ageing public servant, out-of-tune
With his times, oddball growing daily odder,
Allows himself the craziest fantasies,
Sage ruler putting the ancient world to rights!
Then he awakes and sees his outcast state,
Accepting as fact his white-haired worthlessness.
When the coffin lid finally caps these hare-brained schemes,
Only then will these desires come to an end.

Even now I grieve at the sufferings of the poor,
I sigh for them, my insides seethe with rage.
When my former classmates mock my naiveté
I pay them back with poems yet more vehement.
Of course I have wanted to be free at last,
Watching the sunsets in my hermit's cottage;
But I happen to live under an enlightened ruler,
And could not bear to exile myself forever.
17   I know full well the most skilful carpenters
Have already constructed the lofty Mansions of State;
19   But the tiny sunflower yearns for the brilliant sun.
How can I uproot my deepest feelings?

---

17 i.e. government ministers 'building' the state.
19 i.e. *the brilliant sun* is the emperor, whom he yearns to serve.

14

自京赴奉先縣詠懷五百字

杜陵有布衣　取笑同學翁
老大意轉拙　浩歌彌激烈
許身一何愚　竊比稷與契
居然成濩落　白首甘契闊
蓋棺事則已　此志常覬豁
窮年憂黎元　歎息腸內熱

非無江海志　蕭灑送日月
生逢堯舜君　不忍便永訣
當今廊廟具　構廈豈云缺
葵藿傾太陽　物性固難奪

15

And yet I think of the swarm of humble ants,
Each picking a careful track to its cell in the nest.
So why should I emulate the almighty whale,
24 And wallow amongst the waves in arrogance?
    Knowing this, I feel ashamed of my persistence,
    Ashamed that I've pandered to the powerful.
    I've merely proved my insecurity.
    I must bow my head to the dust, obliteration.

    And I think again of those ancient hermits, true
30 To their inner promptings, unsoiled by the world.
    Drink deep, Du Fu, and release yourself a little.
    Sing, rage out loud, dispel your violent grief.

    Narrative

    At the year's end, the grasses die in shreds,
    Winds savagely buffet the cliffs, even split them.
    And in the city, in the dead middle of the night,
    Under a glowering sky, the traveller gets ready to leave.
    Savage frost has stiffened his sash—it tears;
    Fingers frozen stiff as rods can't mend it.

    By dawn he has reached Mount Li, the Winter Palace—
    Up there, near the peaks, couched in imperial splendour—

24: Like arrogant, all-powerful government ministers.
30: The world of politics, that is.

顧惟螻蟻輩
但自求其穴
胡為慕大鯨
輒擬偃溟渤
從茲悟生理
獨恥事干謁
兀兀遂至今
忍為塵埃沒
終愧巢與由
未能易其節

沈飲聊自遣
放歌破愁絕
歲暮百草零
疾風高岡裂
天衢陰崢嶸
客子中夜發
霜嚴衣帶斷
指直不能結
凌晨過驪山
御榻在嶙峋

The freezing sky is filled with army banners,
Passes worn to glass by the constant tramping of feet.
43 A dense mist rises over the bubbling pools,
Ringed by Guards' pikes, which seem to graze each other.
There ruler and subject are drenched in splendid pleasures,
As music ascends the sky in a crescendo.
Hot-spring bathing's for those receiving His favour—
The royal table is not for homespun diners—
49 And each bolt of silk, given out in the crimson courtyard,
Came from the icy loom of a peasant woman.
Her husband had to endure the pitiless lash
To ensure it reached the capital on time.
The bountiful grants from the Imperial coffers—
He clearly desires us all to be well and prosper—
If his ministers fiddle the books and squander his riches—
56 How could He be blamed for abandoning principle?
The court is filled with a wealth of public servants
And the generous ones have real cause to tremble.

In fact I hear the Imperial golden plate
Has all gone to His favourite-in-law, his 'brother'

43: This is the site of one of the few hot springs in China.
49: It was paved with crimson coloured earth.
56: See the next couplet: Du Fu is protesting too loudly.

18

蚩尤塞寒空
蹴踏崖谷滑
瑤池氣鬱律
羽林相摩戛
君臣留歡娛
樂動殷膠葛
賜浴皆長纓
與宴非短褐
彤庭所分帛
本自寒女出

鞭撻其夫家
聚斂貢城闕
聖人筐篚恩
實願邦國活
臣如忽至理
君豈棄此物
多士盈朝廷
仁者宜戰慄
況聞內金盤
盡在衛霍室

His favourite stands vision-like in the court, a goddess,
Shining through silk and the faint mist that surrounds her.
The guests themselves are warmed by sable coats,
To the wistful notes of the lute and the pensive zither.
To entertain them, a broth of camel's hoof,
Bowls fragrant with pungent oranges, tangerines.

Behind the rich man's gates, the obscene stink of feasting.
By the roadside the bones of people who froze to death.
Glorious and wretched, a mere inch apart.
I think of these things, and my heart is filled with despair.

I turn to the North, where the Wei and Jing rivers meet,
72 And find the public ferry's no longer there.
The river in icy spate hurtles down from the west:
Wherever I gaze, the jutting edges of peaks.
75 I fear that Mt Kong itself will come tumbling down,
Crash into the pillars of Heaven and end this world.
At least the rope-way across has not been broken:
Its wooden supports creak in a desperate way.
Clinging to its ropes, we travellers help each other,
The river's so wide, we cannot believe we'll make it.

72: Moved because of high water, etc.
75: The souce of the Wei and Jing rivers.

中堂有神仙
煙霧蒙玉質
煖客貂鼠裘
悲管逐清瑟
勸客駝蹄羹
霜橙壓香橘
朱門酒肉臭
路有凍死骨
榮枯咫尺異
惆悵難再述

北轅就涇渭
官渡又改轍
群冰從西下
極目高崒兀
疑是崆峒來
恐觸天柱折
河梁幸未坼
枝撐聲窸窣
行李相攀援
川廣不可越

I had left my family in this neighbouring province,
Ten people in all, cut off by snowstorms and mountains.
How could I bear to keep on ignoring them?
I was longing to join them, share their hunger and thirst.
I opened the gate and heard a desperate howling:
My youngest son had just then died of hunger.
How could I find an end to my helpless tears?

Our neighbours quietly sobbed in sympathy.
I've failed as their father, I cannot forgive my shame
That I had no scrap of food to ward off his death.
How could I guess, as the autumn harvest ripened,
That poverty would wear them down this far?

For my lifetime I have exemption from paying taxes,
94   My name will not be inscribed in the call-up roster.
Looking back at my tracks, I feel much bitterness:
The ordinary people have yet more cause for anger.
I think, in silence, of those forced off their land,
98   Of those marched off to die in distant battles.
I cower before this mountain of rage and grief,
Not knowing how to begin to make an ending.

94: As an official, Du was automatically exempt.
98: A few days after Du completed this poem, An Lu-shan's rebellion,
which seriously shook, and very nearly ended, the Tang dynasty,
broke out. Some scholars have suggested that Du may have envisaged
some such disaster.

老妻寄異縣
十口隔風雪
誰能久不顧
庶往共饑渴
入門聞號咷
幼子餓已卒
吾寧舍一哀
里巷亦嗚咽
所愧為人父
無食致夭折

豈知秋禾登
貧窶有倉卒
生常免租稅
名不隸征伐
撫跡猶酸辛
平人固騷屑
默思失業徒
因念遠戍卒
憂端齊終南
鴻洞不可掇

FACING A SNOW STORM

Fresh corpses' ghosts sob on the field of battle,
In the city an old man sits alone and chants.
Ragged clouds scud past in the withering light,
Snow dances its hectic flurries in the wind.
In the empty bottle and cup, no glint of wine;
In the stove's dying embers, hope still faintly glows.

Cut off from news and loved ones, in the air
8   He traces Despair in empty characters.

8: This refers to the Chinese habit of tracing characters (where no pen is to hand) with (e.g.) a chopstick on a restaurant table, or with a finger on the palm of one's hand.

對雪

戰哭多新鬼　飄裹樽無綠

愁吟獨老翁　爐存火似紅

亂雲低薄暮　數州消息斷

急雪舞迴風　愁坐正書空

THE YOUNG PRINCE

White-hooded crows flew over the capital,
Perched on the Welcoming Autumn Gate, and cawed,
Pecked tiles off the roofs of the gilded mansions,
Panicked officials into flight from the horde.

Horses were flogged to death in the rout, whips broken,
Fleeing Imperials left their own kin behind:
Madly adorned still, belted with jade and coral,
He stands alone at the corner, weeps for his kind.

Too scared to greet me, he barely answers my questions,
Just begs for shelter, willing to serve as my slave!
For a hundred days he hid like a rat in a hole:
Thorns travelled his body, but he was saved.

The moment I saw that aquiline face, I knew it,
The Imperial features traced in every line!
15   But the Dragon is now in the wild, wolves roam the City,
'You must hide yourself, Sir, try to bide your time.'

'It's much too risky to stand at this corner chatting,
Yet I will briefly tell you what little I know:
Last night in the stink of slaughter the rebels' camels,
Laden with royal plunder, lumbered along the roads.

15: The emperor, in temporary exile.

哀王孫

長安城頭頭白烏
夜飛延秋門上呼
又向人家啄大屋
屋底達官走避胡
金鞭折斷九馬死
骨肉不得同馳驅
腰下寶玦青珊瑚
可憐王孫泣路隅
問之不肯道姓名
但道困苦乞為奴

已經百日竄荊棘
身上無有完肌膚
高帝子孫盡隆準
龍種自與常人殊
豺狼在邑龍在野
王孫善保千金軀
不敢長語臨交衢
且為王孫立斯須
昨夜東風吹血腥
東來橐駝滿舊都

The Northern Veterans, so staunch and strong,
Are now the pathetic butt of rebel jibes.
But also, I've heard, the old emperor's handed on
24 His throne to his son, who won over the Northern Tribes.

These have gashed their faces, sworn revenge or death—
But we must stop whispering words for spies to hear!
Alas, sir, you cannot afford the tiniest slip,
May your ancestors' guardian spirits always be near.

24: The new emperor has 'won over' these barbarian tribes, who will
fight on 'our' side against the rebels.

朔方健兒好身手
昔何勇銳今何愚
竊聞天子已傳位
聖德北服南單于

花門剺面請雪恥
慎勿出口他人狙
哀哉王孫慎勿疎
五陵佳氣無時無

North West Moon

Tonight's moon, over the northern plain,
My wife watches in lonely isolation.
With her our children, pitiful and little,
Gaze at the moon in lost bewilderment.

In the fragrant mist, her cloudlike hair is damp,
In the clear moonlight, her arms gleam white and cold.
Oh when shall we two stand by the open window
Drying our joyful tears by the light of this moon?

月夜

今夜鄜州月
閨中只獨看
遙憐小兒女
未解憶長安

香霧雲鬟濕
清輝玉臂寒
何時倚虛幌
雙照淚痕乾

SPRING VIEW

The ruins of state   mountains and rivers
This city in spring   grasses, trees wild.
Season-buffeted   flowers shed tears
Anguished at parting   birds screech alarm.
Lookout beacons   flash fire for months
Letter from home   would be gold.
White head hairs   scratched nearly bald:
8   Soon quite unworthy   of a hatpin!

8: Chinese at this time did their hair up in a topknot, which was used to hold their (hat and) hatpin.

春望

國破山河在
城春草木深
感時花濺淚
恨別鳥驚心

烽火連三月
家書抵萬金
白頭搔更短
渾欲不勝簪

Venting My Feelings

Last year when the rebels sacked the capital,
They parted me from wife and family.
This year, in summer's rich increase,
I slipped through enemy lines, fled to the west.
I reached the court, came before His Majesty
In hempen sandals, both elbows poking through!
The courtiers welcomed back this living ghost,
My friends saw how I'd aged, and pitied me.
9 In tears I received the title of Omissioner:
A gracious response to me in my wretched state.

I might have petitioned for leave to return to my family,
But could not bring myself to speak out of turn.
13 I sent a letter to their village asking for news,
Not even knowing if they still existed.
Then I heard the whole district was trapped in disaster:
The savages slaughtered even the dogs and chickens!

9: Whose job was to remind the emperor of matters he had omitted
to attend to.
13, and 25–26: Du refers in this poem to two letters. The first to be
referred to, in line 13, is a recent attempt to elicit some information
about his family. The next one mentioned, in lines 25–26, was an
earlier effort, sent 'ten long months' ago.

述懷

去年潼關破
妻子隔絕久
今夏草木長
脱身得西走
麻鞋見天子
衣袖見兩肘
朝庭愍生還
親故傷老醜

涕淚受拾遺
流離主恩厚
柴門雖得去
未忍即開口
寄書問三川
不知家在否
比聞同罹禍
殺戮到雞狗

In the mountains, under the dripping straw of our thatch
Who will be left to wait for me at the door?
Their bodies smashed, at the foot of the flourishing pines,
They lie on the frozen ground and stare at us.
How many people escaped the rebels' onslaught?
How could all my family have survived?
There, up on the peaks, where hungry tigers prowl—
My heart's in knots, I twist my head round and look.
I actually dread the coming of news from them:
How can my heart withstand yet more disaster?

25 Since I sent them that letter, when hiding in the capital,
26 Ten long months have already passed.
But our mighty Empire, resurgent, revives itself,
I drink with my usual joy to imperial splendour,
Dreading, as I join in the general rejoicing,
That I am facing a poor and lonely old age.

山中焗茅屋　囙寄一封書
誰復依戶牖　今已十月後
推頹蒼松根　寸心亦何有
地冷骨未朽　仅畏消息來
幾人全性命　漢運初中興
盡室營桐隅　生平老耽酒
歆岑猛虎場　沈思歡會處
鬱結迴我首　恐作窮獨叟

THE GREAT TREK NORTH

Introduction

In the second year of our new emperor's reign,
In autumn, on the lucky first of the month,
Du Fu prepared to make his great trek north,
To seek his family in the vast confusion.
The times indeed were full of anguish and worry,
At court, in the country: no-one free for a second.
Which is why I was so moved by the emperor's kindness,
Granting me permission to visit my thatched hut again.
I went to the palace gate for my leave-taking,
But lingered a long time, quite unable to leave.
11 For although I lack the true talent of an Omissioner,
I fear His Majesty might still omit some thing.
His Majesty breathes new life into the empire,
Bends his mind over the delicate pattern of things.
But the Eastern barbarian hordes are still on the rampage,
16 Which cuts me, your humble subject, to the quick.

11: Whose job (as in p34, line 9) was to remind the emperor of
matters he had omitted to attend to.
16: Du Fu may well have intended this poem for the emperor's eyes.

北征

皇帝二載秋
閏八月初吉
杜子將北征
蒼茫問家室
維時遭艱虞
朝野少暇日
顧慚恩私被
詔許歸蓬蓽

拜辭詣闕下
怵惕久未出
雖乏諫諍姿
恐君有遺失
君誠中興主
經緯固密勿
東胡反未已
臣甫憤所切

I wipe away tears, look back at the Provisional Palace,
Look ahead at the road which blurs into the distance.
All the earth bears the terrible scars of war.
Will our fears and anxieties ever come to an end?

Narrative

Step by painful step we slog through the mud:
A lonely landscape bare of people and wood-smoke.
Those we do meet are mostly the victims of war:
Their cold wounds have re-opened and ooze agony.
I turn my head, look back at Fengxiang District,
Flags ripple in evening sunlight, then suddenly vanish.

I advance again, climb folds of freezing mountains,
Stumble across some ancient watering holes.
Our path dips down as we approach the next town,
The river roils madly in the valley down there.
Fierce tigers block the path in front of me:
They roar, the green green cliffs are split apart.
Chrysanthemums droop petals acknowledging autumn,
Rocks bear pock-marks from ancient waggon wheels.
Clouds puff good cheer against a brilliant blue:
Such carefree artistry makes my spirits soar!

揮涕戀行在
道途猶恍惚
乾坤含瘡痍
憂虞何時畢
靡靡踰阡陌
人煙眇蕭瑟
所遇多被傷
呻吟更流血
回首鳳翔縣
旌旗晚明滅

前登寒山重
屢得飲馬窟
邠郊入地底
涇水中盪潏
猛虎立我前
蒼崖吼時裂
菊垂今秋花
石戴古車轍
青雲動高興
幽事亦可悅

Millions of tiny mountain berries hanging
Trellised by acorn branches and chestnut leaves:
Some crimson, like the crystals of cinnabar,
Some jet-black berries, carelessly spattered lacquer.
All those which rain and dew so richly moisten,
Sweet and bitter, they equally bear fruit.
43 I think of that distant Paradise, Peach Blossom Spring,
And sigh at the ugly clumsiness of my world.

As we rise and fall on the path, a hill-shrine:
To us on ridges, in valleys, it comes and goes.
I've already rushed right down to its river bank,
My servant hangs at the trees' end, high up the slope.
Owls hoot amongst the yellowing mulberry leaves,
Mountain rats squat on their haunches greeting us.
In the depths of the night we pass a battlefield,
See bleached bones shining in the pale moonlight.
At the Tong Pass a host of a million men
Just recently was scattered in sudden confusion.
Following this, half the men of that province
56 Suffered grievous harm, were terribly transformed.

43: A kind of Shangri-la which, as the name suggests, was a land of
innocent plenty.
56: i.e. killed. This is the disastrous defeat referred to in 'Facing a
Snow Storm' (p24).

山果多瑣細
羅生雜橡栗
或紅如丹砂
或黑如點漆
雨露之所濡
甘苦齊結實
緬思桃源內
益歎身世拙
坡陀望鄜畤
巖谷互出沒

我行已水濱
我僕猶木末
鴟鳥鳴黃桑
野鼠拱亂穴
夜深經戰場
寒月照白骨
潼關百萬師
往者散何卒
遂令半秦民
殘害為異物

57   And I, for my part, fell into barbarian dust,
      Now I return my head quite grizzled with grey.
      It took me a year to get to our thatched hut,
      And find our family clothed in a quiltwork of patches.
      The pine woods echo our sobs of joy and grief,
      The mountain stream chokes mournfully over its rocks.
      My little lad, whose pranks I always loved,
      Has a face which hunger has blanched whiter than snow.
      Seeing his daddy he turns his back and howls:
      I see his filthy feet are completely bare.
      In front of my bed my two youngest daughters
      Wear stitches and patches that barely cover their knees:
      The waves of the seascape have been pulled apart
      To be filled with a jumble of old embroidered cloth:
      Leviathan and Purple Phoenix, once at the centre,
      Now take a nose-dive down to the bottom hem.

      The head of this family's overwhelmed with feelings,
      He pukes and shits, couch-bound for several days.
      But then he rallies, and yes, he has new silk cloth
      To keep you, my darlings, from shivering from cold.

57: As noted in the Appendix (ref. poems on pages 26–34), Du was
captured and taken to the rebel-occupied capital, Chang'an.

況我墮胡塵
及歸盡華髮
經年至茅屋
妻子衣百結
慟哭松聲迴
悲泉共幽咽
平生所嬌兒
顏色白勝雪
見耶背面啼
垢膩腳不襪

牀前兩小女
補綻才過膝
海圖拆波濤
舊繡移曲折
天吳及紫鳳
顛倒在裋褐
老夫情懷惡
嘔泄臥數日
那無囊中帛
救汝寒凜慄

He also unpacks make-up from his bags,
Spread out, in tiny parcels, on our bedding.
My wife's thinned face glows with a sudden light,
My youngest daughters struggle to comb their hair.
Copying mum there's nothing they will not try,
Smearing her morning make-up all over their faces.
In a moment they've applied powder and rouge,
Adorning eyebrows with widely erring liner.
To return alive and play with these dear children
Almost drives out thoughts of hunger and thirst.
They all tug at my beard, pepper me with questions:
How could I bear to shout at them for this?
Thinking back to my despair among the rebels
I can happily bear this riotous, noisy screeching.
I've decided on a short holiday from worry:
Making a living can wait a day or two!

His majesty is still begrimed with the dust of war.
When will he be able to rest from training troops?
I look up at Heaven: its complexion is on the turn:
I *feel* the baleful colours are draining away.

粉黛亦解苞

袈裯稍羅列

瘦妻面復光

癡女頭自櫛

學母無不為

曉妝隨手抹

移時施朱鉛

狼藉畫眉闊

生還對童稚

似欲忘饑渴

問事競挽鬚

誰能即嗔喝

翻思在賊愁

甘受雜亂聒

新歸且慰意

生理焉得說

至尊尚蒙塵

幾日休練卒

仰觀天色改

坐覺妖氛豁

An icy wind is blowing from the North West,
98 Bringing panic and death in the wake of Uighur warriors.
Their king has sworn obedience and assistance.
Swoop down and kill: such is the life they know.
They have sent five thousand of their bravest men,
102 Driving ten thousand rider-less horses before them.
103 What they prize is the first flush of valiant youth.
The whole world bows to their totally ruthless daring.
These people will soar like eagles over their prey,
Burst quicker than arrows through the enemy ranks.
Our emperor awaits victory with a tranquil mind;
We lesser mortals talk about them, and tremble.
109 The Eastern Capital's in the palm of our hands,
110 The Western Capital can be left till later.
Our government troops must strike them—hard and deep!
With Uighur help release your pent-up energy!
Our first onslaught will recapture the far North East,
And soon the neighbouring provinces will fall.
In the depths of Heaven frost and snow are forming:
Piles of freezing white death massing on high.

98: Barbarians (ie non-Chinese) who had been persuaded to fight
against the 'Eastern barbarians' who are mentioned in line 15
as being still in rebellion.
102: As spare mounts, or to supplement government cavalry. Chinese
armies were often short of horses, which tended to be bought from
the nomads of central Asia.
103: Unlike Chinese, who prize seniority.
109: Loyang.
110: Chang'an, modern Xi'an.

陰風西北來
慘澹隨回紇
其王顧助順
其俗善馳突
送兵五千人
驅馬一萬匹
此輩少為貴
四方服勇決
所用皆鷹騰
破敵過箭疾

聖心頗虛佇
時議氣欲奪
伊洛指掌收
西京不足拔
官軍請深入
蓄銳可俱發
此舉開青徐
旋瞻略恆碣
昊天積霜露
正氣有肅殺

The Wheel of Fate revolves, to their dismay,
It has come to pass: this month will ensnare them.
Barbarian fortune—how could it last forever?
The pattern of our lives will be renewed.

I remember the past, when the present Troubles started,
We managed affairs much better than the ancients!
Our traitors were chopped into mincemeat, food for dogs,
Their comrades-in-evil suffered a similar fate.
When the ancient dynasties faced such a crisis,
126 Their rulers spared the parasites, their favourites,
But more recently, both the Zhou and Han dynasties,
Saw emperors brilliant enough to renew our lives.
Hardened and brave, our present general
Brandishes his splendid battle-axe.
We truly believed the rebels would slaughter us all;
Now our triumphant dynasty rises again.

Not a single footfall in the Palace of Great Harmony,
White Tiger Hall is stilled with loneliness.
135 But the citizens scan the horizon for the Rainbow Banner,
The Golden Gateway shines brightly with new life.

126: The idea here is of imperial favourites who use their privileged
position to ruin the government.
135-6: The emperor's banner. He hasn't literally returned—see line
110 and note above—but the citizens' (and Du Fu's) yearning for this
makes it feel imminent, and the Golden Gateway is already infused
(so to speak) with the Imperial presence.

禍轉亡胡歲
勢成擒胡月
胡命其能久
皇綱未宜絕
憶昨狼狽初
事與古先別
姦臣竟葅醢
同惡隨蕩析
不聞夏殷衰
中自誅褒妲

周漢獲再興
宣光果明哲
桓桓陳將軍
仗鉞奮忠烈
微爾人盡非
於今國猶活
淒涼大同殿
寂寞白獸闥
都人望翠華
佳氣向金闕

The spirits of imperial ancestors, in their mounds,
Guard us: we shall never neglect their graves.
The Founding Emperor's Enterprise glitters anew.
He set it broad and deep, to shelter us for ever.

園陵固有神
掃灑數不缺
煌煌太宗業
樹立甚宏達

THREE POEMS WRITTEN AT CHIANG VILLAGE

I

From towering pinnacles of fiery cloud
The slanting sun casts shafts of light on the plain.
A crowd of sparrows brawls at the rickety gate,
As the wanderer walks the last of his 300 miles.
Wife and children, shocked with disbelief,
Calm a little, then again burst into tears.
"A world of turmoil—tossed about like a feather;
My returning alive—an accidental achievement."
The faces of our neighbours line the earthen wall:
Sighing sadly they shed tears of sympathy.
Well past midnight, my wife and I both hold candles,
Each of us gazing at the phantom other.

II

Late in my years I filched a second life:
Now, a survivor, I have little relish for living.
My playful son refuses to leave my knee,
Fearing that I will desert him once again.
I remember the past, catching the cool of these trees,
As we followed them in their circle round the lake.
Now the North wind whirls its angry rhetoric
And the constant, gnawing anxiety of our cares.

羌村三首

一

崢嶸赤雲西
日腳下平地
柴門鳥雀噪
歸客千里至
妻孥怪我在
驚定還拭淚
世亂遭飄蕩
生還偶然遂
鄰人滿牆頭
感歎亦歔欷
夜闌更秉燭
相對如夢寐

二

晚歲迫偷生
還家少歡趣
嬌兒不離膝
畏我復卻去
憶昔好追涼
故繞池邊樹
蕭蕭北風勁
撫事煎百慮

At least the wheat and millet have all been harvested,
The fermenting mash is dripping its alcohol.
So for now it's enough to measure out a drink.
Perhaps this will console my declining years.

III

The hens start up a raucous clamour of squawking,
Turning, as visitors come, to open warfare.
I chase the noisome birds into the trees,
Only then hear the knocking at my gate.
Four or five of the eldest of our neighbours
Have come to greet me, home from my far-flung travels.
Each of them has in his hands an offering:
I empty the pitchers, we try the different drinks.
"Please accept our rather insipid brews,
The arable land has no-one left to plough it;
Since the wars go on, the fighting has not stopped,
Our sons have all been marched off to the East."
I beg the old men to accept a song in return,
Feeling ashamed of their sympathy, their suffering.
When my song is done, we look up to Heaven and sigh,
And the faces of all of us are wet with tears.

賴知禾黍收，手中各有攜。

已覺糟粃注，傾榼溜復清。

如今足斟酌，莫辭酒味薄。

且用慰遲暮，黍地無人耕。

三

羣鷄正亂叫，兵革既未息。

客至鷄鬭爭，兒童盡東征。

驅鷄上樹木，請為父老歌。

怜聞叩柴荊，艱難愧深情。

父老四五人，歌罷仰天嘆。

問我久遠行，四座淚縱橫。

SPRING NIGHT IN THE IMPERIAL PALACE

Blossoms shadow the garden walls,
Twittering birds fly home to rest.
Stars shimmer over the thousand doors,
And the moon ascends in the deep sky.

Unable to sleep, I hear the great doors creak open,
Imagine the breeze tinkling the bridle bells.
I must attend the morning reception tomorrow,
And again I ask, 'What time of night is it?'

春宿左省

花隱掖垣暮
啾啾棲鳥過
星臨萬戶動
月傍九霄多

不寢聽金鑰
因風想玉珂
明朝有封事
數問夜如何

Two Verses Written by the Serpentine*

I

Every falling petal tears a little away from spring—
Ten thousand whirling in the wind, just to make us sad.
See the end of the blossoms as they pass through our gaze
And do not grudge cup upon cup of wine.

The little pavilion on the island harbours a pair of kingfishers,
6   On the high mound beside the park—a snoozing unicorn.
Analyse the Cause of Things, and strive for enjoyment;
Why snare yourself in the search for a vanishing name?

II

Returning from court day after day I pawn a few more
    spring clothes,
And every day go home to my hut by the river utterly drunk.
Wine-debts I have in plenty at the drinking shops I go to—
How many have lived to seventy from ancient times till now?

In and out of the countless flowers the butterflies thread
    their way,
And dragonflies skim lazily over the water.
I say to this spring scene: 'Let us flow together
A little while, not distance each other so.'

---

* This was an artificial lake in a famous beauty spot on the edge of
Ch'ang-an, the then capital of China.
6: The 'mound' is a grave-mound, the unicorn a stone statue.

曲江二首

一

一片花飛減却春
風飄萬點正愁人
且看欲盡花經眼
莫厭傷多酒入脣
江上小堂巢翡翠
苑邊高塚臥麒麟
細推物理須行樂
何用浮名絆此身

二

朝回日日典春衣
每日江頭盡醉歸
酒債尋常行處有
人生七十古來稀
穿花蛺蝶深深見
點水蜻蜓款款飛
傳語風光共流轉
暫時相賞莫相違

61

For My Friend Wei Ba, Living in Retirement

We poor humans seem to live
Like stars whose orbits never meet.
So how come now, this evening, here
We share the flickering lamp light?

Then strong and young, did we not see
Our temples now, quite flecked with grey?
So many mutual friends deceased—
We cry aloud in shock. Death stings.

You, twenty years ago unwed,
Now, as I climb towards your home,
Line up your grinning boys and girls
To greet their father's long-lost friend.

They smile at me, as children should,
Politely ask me where I'm from.
Their anxious father interrupts,
And urges them to bring us wine.

贈衞八處士

人生不相見
動如參與商
今夕復何夕
共此燈燭光
少壯能幾時
鬢髮各已蒼
訪舊半為鬼
驚呼熱中腸

焉知二十載
重上君子堂
昔別君未婚
兒女忽成行
怡然敬父執
問我來何方
問答未及已
驅兒羅酒漿

Outside, in the rainy dark, spring chives are cut,
And fresh-steamed rice gleams with yellow millet.

My host exclaims 'It's hard to meet . . . '
And we are soon ten glasses gone.
Ten glasses! Yet my head's still clear
Because our friendship is so strong.

And yet, tomorrow's sun will shine
On each old friend on a different side of the mountain,
Lost in the hopeless busyness of life.

夜雨剪春韭

新炊間黃粱

主稱會面難

一舉累十觴

十觴亦不醉

感子故意長

明日隔山岳

世事兩茫茫

FOR MY GUEST

South of my hut, North of my hut, spring waters play,
The gulls, who favour those without guile, come often.
The path to my door's crazed over by brilliant flowers,
And now for the first time I open my gate to a guest!
We're far from the market, our cooking is quite simple,
My family's poor, our home-brew's not that fresh.
But if you're willing to drink with my goodly neighbour
I'll call over to him to finish a jar with us.

客至

舍南舍北皆春水
但見羣鷗日日來
花徑不曾緣客掃
蓬門今始為君開

盤飧市遠無兼味
樽酒家貧只舊醅
肯與鄰翁相對飲
隔籬呼取盡餘杯

Spring Night and a Gift of Rain

The fine rain   knows its season
Pairs with spring   brings forth life.
Faintest drops   wafted by night
Soak every thing   in silent detail.
Over country paths clouds mass darkly
On a single boat   lamp-light glints.
Morning reveals   drenched in red
8 Deep in flowers   Chengdu, City of Silk

8: So called because it used to make an annual tax payment of silk brocade (a local product).

春夜喜雨

好雨知時節

當春乃發生

隨風潛入夜

潤物細無聲

野徑雲俱黑

江船火獨明

曉看紅濕處

花重錦官城

RIVERSIDE PAVILION

Spread-eagled on warm ground   this suits me to a T
Singing deep and long   I survey the scene.
River flowing past   heart doesn't compete
Clouds hanging up there   mind stills as well.
Silently splendid   spring's on the wane
Rejoicing in thisness   all is itself.
To my nest in the old wood   having failed to return
Dispelling grief   I force myself to write.

江亭

坦腹江亭暖
長吟野望時
水流心不競
雲在意俱遲

寂寂春將晚
欣欣物自私
故林歸未得
排悶強裁詩

As It Comes: *Nine Glimpses of Spring*

1

Although she can see me sunk in untimely grief
Shameless spring still comes with her gaudy revels.
She showers the blossoms down in a frenzied flurry,
Rouses golden orioles to sing the livelong day.

2

I planted these peach and plum trees in their rows
By this low earthen wall which marks out my land.
It seems the spring has come to exploit my weakness:
A thief in the night, it's robbed some boughs of their blossoms.

3

Knowing full well I live in a lowly hut
The swallows come here from the river deliberately,
Bespattering lute and books with mud from their beaks
Chasing insects that flee and then bump into me!

4

The third month's gone, the fourth is now here,
I sink into old age greeting spring again.
Do not bother with the Infinite beyond;
Make do with this world's finite cup of wine!

絕句漫興九首

眼見客愁愁不醒
無賴春色到江亭
即遣花開深造次
便覺鶯語太丁寧
右一

手種桃李非無主
野老牆低還是家
恰似春風相欺得
夜來吹折數枝花

右二

熟知茅齋絕低小
江上燕子故來頻
銜泥點污琴書內
更接飛蟲打著人
右三

二月已破三月來
漸老逢春能幾回
莫思身外無窮事
且盡生前有限杯

73

5

Heart's ache—the river's spring spate is nearly gone;
I hobble beside it, pause by the flower-rich island.
Crazy tufts of willow-down whirl on the breeze,
Fickle peach blossoms float away with the current.

6

Too lazy to be any use, I stay in the village,
In spite of broad daylight I close the gate to my hut.
On vivid moss, with cloudy wine, in this forest clearing:
Blue river, spring breeze, and the distant landscape darkening.

7

Willow down spreads a smooth carpet over the path,
Lotus leaves are green coins poured over the stream.
Among sprouting bamboos a pheasant chick struts unnoticed,
On the sand-bank ducklings sound asleep by their mother.

8

West of my hut the mulberry leaves can be plucked,
On the river bank the wheat stalks are young and delicate.
What's old age worth as spring turns into summer?
Let's not forget the fragrant, honey-sweet brew!

腸斷春江欲盡頭
杖藜徐步立芳洲
顛狂柳絮隨風去
輕薄桃花逐水流

右五

懶慢無堪不出村
呼兒日在掩柴門
蒼苔濁酒林中靜
碧水春風野外香

右六

糝逕楊花鋪白氈
點溪荷葉疊青錢
筍根稚子無人見
沙上鳧雛傍母眠

右七

舍西柔桑葉可拈
江畔細麥復纖纖
人生幾何春已夏
不放香醪如蜜甜

9

Just outside my door the willow tendrils sway
Like the pliable waists of fifteen year-old girls.
Who'd dare to claim that with dawn he had not noticed
The mad wind blew in last night, snapped off the longest?

右八

隔戶楊柳弱嫋嫋
恰似十五女兒腰
雖謂朝來不作意
狂風挽斷最長條

右九

MY THATCHED HUT SMASHED BY THE AUTUMN WIND

At the peak of autumn the wind howled furiously,
Ripped all three layers of thatch from off my roof,
Tossed it in cartwheels to the far side of the river:
High up, in tufts, it trimmed the edge of the forest,
Lower down its wisps skimmed circles on the puddles.
The lads from the village exploited my age and weakness.
Now ruthless pilferers, right in front of my eyes
They gathered whole armfuls, slipped into the tall bamboos,
Leaving me to shout myself hoarse, to no effect,
Then hobble home on my stick to moan at my luck.

The wind now dropped, clouds darkened to inky purple,
A thick pall over the whole of the autumn sky.
My cotton coverlet, already thin, iron-cold—
My son in his nightmare kicked its lining to pieces.
The roof now leaks over every part of my bed,
Rain comes through straight as grain stalks, will not stop.

茅屋為秋風所破歌

八月秋高風怒號　脣焦口燥呼不得

卷我屋上三重茅　歸來倚杖自嘆息

茅飛渡江灑江郊　俄頃風定雲墨色

高者掛罥長林梢　秋天漠漠向昏黑

下者飄轉沈塘坳　布衾多年冷似鐵

南村群童欺我老無力　嬌兒惡臥踏裏裂

忍能對面為盜賊　牀頭屋漏無乾處

公然抱茅入竹去　雨脚如麻未斷絕

Since we survived the recent slaughter sleep has been scarce;
Still harder, soaked and cold, to get through each night.

I wish I could build a hall of a million rooms
To house the whole world's freezing scholars and give them joy,
Sheltered from wind and rain, as safe as a mountain.
If I could only see this structure rising high before my eyes
I'd gladly freeze to death inside this wrecked hut.

自經喪亂少睡眠

長夜沾濕何由徹

安得廣廈千萬間

大庇天下寒士俱歡顏

風雨不動安如山

嗚呼

何時眼前突兀見此屋

吾廬獨破受凍死亦足

On Hearing the Imperial Army Has Defeated the Rebels

At the edge of the world we suddenly hear: they're defeated!
I realise my sleeve is soaked with tears.
What's happened to those glum faces—my wife and children?
Happy out of my mind, I shuffle and pack my books.

Sing out loud to the bright sun: do your duty: DRINK;
I'll take spring with me on my way back home.
I can soar like a bird at last on its way to the nest
Skimming the peaks of the Yangtze Gorges, back to Loyang.

聞官軍收河南河北

劍外忽傳收薊北　　　初聞涕淚滿衣裳
卻看妻子愁何在　　　漫卷詩書喜欲狂

白首放歌須縱酒　　　青春作伴好還鄉
即從巴峽穿巫峽　　　便下襄陽向洛陽

83

Two Glimpses of Spring

1

Slow sunlight   river and mountains sparkle,
Spring breeze   flowers and grasses scented;
Melting mud   soars swallows to build a nest,
Warm sandbank   snoozes pairs of mandarin ducks.

2

River emerald   birds whiter still,
Mountains light-green flowers nearly ablaze;
Glance at spring   and see it already gone.
O when shall I   get back to my home in the North?

絕句二首

一

遲日江山麗

春風花草香

泥融飛燕子

沙暖睡鴛鴦

二

江碧鳥逾白

山青花欲然

今春看又過

何日是歸年

This Wearisome Night

Cold rustles bamboos   and infiltrates my room
Moon over the moor   fills the whole courtyard.
Dew thickens   to drops at the end of leaves
Sparse stars   flicker then disappear.
Secret in flight   fireflies light themselves
Water roosting   birds call to each other.
All these things   in the endless chaos of war:
Pointless to grieve   as the clear night advances.

倦夜

竹涼侵臥內
野月滿庭隅
重露成涓滴
稀星乍有無

暗飛螢自照
水宿鳥相呼
萬事干戈裏
空悲清夜徂

WRITTEN AT NIGHT WHEN TRAVELLING

Fine grasses   ruffled by breeze
Tall mast   lone boat moored by the bank.
Stars overhang   the unending plain
Moon bobs   in water's moving mass.
Achieve fame   through beautiful words?
Public office?   Too old and ill.
What's he like   this hapless wanderer?
A seagull drifting   between Heaven and Earth.

旅夜書懷

細草微風岸
危檣獨夜舟
星垂平野闊
月湧大江流

名豈文章著
官應老病休
飄飄何所似
天地一沙鷗

SONG OF THE ANCIENT CYPRESS TREE

1   In front of his shrine, an age-old cypress tree,
    Branches perfect as bronze, roots gnarled rock-solid.
    Its girth of forty spans has a frosty rinse;
    Jet-black, sky-piercing, it soars two thousand feet.
5   Prince and chief minister have had their day,
    But the cypress tree's still here for us to admire.
7   Clouds form at its tips, join with the mists of the Gorge,
    In the moonlight it's chilled by the distant Snowy Mountains.

    I remember when I lived in the Brocade Pavilion
10 Prince and his general shared a memorial shrine.
    That cypress framed the ancient plain in its branches,
    Where gaudy paintwork adorned eerily empty windows.
    But this one's clamped to the ground, it's rooted in rock,
    In the depths of the sky it braves the harsh winds alone.
    Only a divine power could keep it up there,
    The Creator himself must have planted it so straight.

1, 5, 10: The 'he' of line 1 is Du Fu's hero Zhu Ge-liang, a 'chief minister/general' who tried to aid a rather lacklustre ruler—the Prince of lines 5 and 10—in his attempts to re-unify China at the end of the Han dynasty. Du Fu frequently refers to Zhu in his verse, and clearly identified with him.
7: The Wu Gorge, one of the famous Yangtze Gorges.
10: This shrine was near Du Fu's pavilion by the Brocade River, a tributary of the Yangtze, near his thatched hut.

古柏行

孔明廟前有老柏
柯如青銅根如石
霜皮溜雨四十圍
黛色參天二千尺
君臣已與時際會
樹木猶為人愛惜
雲來氣接巫峽長
月出寒通雪山白

憶昨路遶錦亭東
先主武侯同閟宮
崔嵬枝幹郊原古
窈窕丹青戶牖空
落落盤踞雖得地
冥冥孤高多烈風
扶持自是神明力
正直原因造化功

Supposing we felled it to build a lofty palace,
Ten thousand yoked oxen would cower before it in wonder:
No signs of human artifice, an artistic marvel,
It's indifferent to felling, too gargantuan to be moved.
Its bitter heart, of course, is teeming with ants,
Its scented branches have sheltered many a phoenix.
The exiled scholar, the lonely hermit, should not be resentful:
From ancient times outstanding talent has flourished unused.

大廈如傾要棟樑
萬牛迴首邱山重
不露文章世已驚
未辭剪伐誰能送

苦心豈免容螻蟻
香葉終經宿鸞鳳
志士幽人莫怨嗟
古來材大難為用

A Night at West House*

Yin and Yang, in the year's evening, hasten the long shadows,
Frost and snow at the edge of Heaven have cleared: cold
    is the night.
3 At the fifth watch the drums and bugles are sadly plangent,
4 Over the Three Gorges, the veil of the Milky Way shimmers.
In the country they are weeping at news of the fighting
While fishermen and woodcutters are singing their uncouth
    songs.
7 Slumbering Dragon and Leaping Horse at last are yellow dust:
Idle to care about letters or men's affairs, idle to moan.

---

*Du Fu wrote this when staying at 'West House', a public building in
Kui-zhou. When he wrote it, there had been civil disturbances in the
area for about a year.

3: 5th watch: about 3–5 am.
4: The Three Gorges—a famous beauty spot—are in this area.
7: Slumbering Dragon, Leaping Horse: nicknames of two generals
who tried unsuccessfully to re-unite a China then split into mini-states.
Both started their campaigns from this area.

閣夜

歲暮陰陽催短景
天涯霜雪霽寒宵
五更鼓角聲悲壯
三峽星河影動搖

野哭千家聞戰伐
夷歌數處起漁樵
臥龍躍馬終黃土
人事音書漫寂寥

CONTEXTUAL BACKGROUND[1]
(page nos. in brackets after poem titles)

755, year-end: Du Fu leaves capital, Chang'an, journeys to Fengxian[2] to see his family: **Five Hundred Words** (page 14). Just after this, An Lu-shan's rebellion breaks out in Northeast China.

756 Rebels inflict severe defeats on the Imperial armies; emperor flees capital Chang'an. Du Fu takes family further north for safety, then tries to reach the emperor's temporary HQ but is captured en route by rebels. Taken to Chang'an: forced to live in the occupied capital: **Facing a Snowstorm** (24), **The Young Prince** (26), **NW Moon** (30).

757, spring: Du still in Chang'an: **Spring View** (32). Escapes, makes way to emperor's temporary HQ, given official position in recognition of bravery: **Venting my Feelings** (34). Told to visit family: **The Great Trek North** (38). Reaches his family: **Three Poems written at Chiang Village** (54). Rebels pushed back from cities of Chang'an and Loyang. Emperor re-enters Chang'an.

758 Du has minor post in Chang'an: **Spring Night in the Imperial Palace** (58), **Two Verses written by the Serpentine** (60). Demoted to minor post in Huazhou.

759 Journeys to Huazhou: **For my Friend Wei Ba, living in retirement** (62). Moves to far NW China with family in search of food. Moves at year-end to Chengdu[3], in SW China.

760 Builds his Thatched Hut in village near Chengdu: **For my Guest** (66).

---

[1] For more detail of the context of each poem, see the *Appendix* (next section).

761 Mostly at Thatched Hut: **Spring Night and a Gift of Rain** (68); **Riverside Pavilion** (70); **As It Comes: Nine Glimpses of Spring** (72), **My Thatched Hut Smashed by the Autumn Wind** (78).

763 An Lu-shan's rebellion finally defeated: **On Hearing the Imperial Army...** (82). AFTER 763: Local disorders continue: Du first at Thatched Hut, later at Kuizhou[4]. **Two Glimpses of Spring** (84), **This Wearisome Night** (86), **Written at Night when Travelling** (88), **Song of the Ancient Cypress Tree** (90), **A Night at West House** (94).

---

[2] 80 miles NE of the capital, Chang'an, where he had been previously.
[3] Upper reaches of river Yangtze.
[4] Near the Yangtze gorges.

APPENDIX

Page Number:

14 **Five Hundred Words:** *Du wrote this poem in 755 AD, when he had finally managed to become a (very minor) official. The journey was to join his wife and children, whom he had already moved to Fengxian (and where he was to take up office).*

24 **Facing a Snowstorm:** *at the time of this poem, the country was being torn apart by civil war, and the rebels had just defeated the government forces and taken over the capital. Soon after, Du Fu— fortunately able to conceal his identity as a government official— was captured and forced to stay in the capital, Chang'an.*

26 **The Young Prince:** *again written whilst Du Fu was in the capital.*

30 **North West Moon:** *same time and place as the previous poem. Du had previously taken his family to a distant village to be safe from the fighting. This poem was written at the time of the annual Mid-Autumn festival, usually celebrated by the whole family.*

32 **Spring View:** *same time and place as the previous poem.*

34 **Venting my feelings:** *when Du Fu wrote this poem he had just escaped from the capital still occupied by the rebels, and somehow managed to make his way to the Emperor's military base some distance away. Here he was welcomed and given a minor post, as a reward for his loyalty.*

38 **The Great Trek North:** *Du wrote this poem when the emperor gave him permission to visit his wife and family. Previous to this, he had escaped from rebel-occupied Chang-an and managed to reach the emperor's Provisional Head Quarters at Fengxiang.*

54 **Three Poems written at Chiang Village:** *by the time he wrote this poem, Du had escaped from the rebel-occupied capital,*

and had somehow accomplished the '300-mile' journey alone, to arrive, out of the blue, on his family's doorstep.

58 **Spring Night in the Imperial Palace:** *by now the rebels were on the retreat, and the emperor had regained his capital city, Chang'an (modern Xi'an). Du Fu was now a minor official. Like other officials, he had to be ready in (very) good time for the dawn reception.*

60 **Two Verses Written by the Serpentine:** *same time and place as previous poem.*

62 **For my friend Wei Ba, Living in Retirement:** *Du was sent to the Eastern Capital, Loyang, on official business, and this probably enabled him to visit Wei Ba. Soon after this, Du gave up public office and spent much of this year in NW China, desperately searching with his family for food. At the end of the same year, he moved to the Chengdu area, on the the upper reaches of the Yangtze.*

66 **For my Guest:** *Du welcomes a guest to his newly built Thatched Hut, near Chengdu.*

68 **Spring Night and a Gift of Rain:** *Du was living at this time in his Thatched Hut.*

70 **Riverside Pavilion:** *same circumstances as the previous poem. The Riverside Pavilion was near his Thatched Hut.*

72 **As It Comes, Nine Glimpses of Spring:** *same circumstances as the previous poem.*

78 **My Thatched Hut Smashed by the Autumn Wind:** *same as the previous poem.*

82 **On Hearing the Imperial Army has defeated the rebels:** *speaks for itself.*

Printed in December 2022
by Rotomail Italia S.p.A., Vignate (MI) - Italy